Contents

In 1987 Jack Buck was awarded the Ford C. Frick Award at the National Baseball Hall of Fame in Cooperstown, NY for his contributions to the game of baseball.

Chicago Radio Hall of Fame Speech

Sunday, October 29, 1995

Thank you, ladies and gentlemen. Thank you, Mike Roarty and Harry Caray, two of my very best friends, and good evening.

I have been given 90 seconds to tell you how proud I am to accept this award and this honor. I can't even think of the names of my kids in 90 seconds...but I do accept this honor on behalf of Bob Hyland, Sam Diggs, Dick Brescia, Frank Miller, Rod Zimmerman, Bob Kipperman, Frank Murphy, Anheuser-Busch, KMOX Radio, the Cardinals, CBS, my family and everyone who ever heard me speak on the radio. I am grateful for the bat of Stan Musial, the arm of Bob Gibson, the legs of Lou Brock and the glove of Ozzie Smith.

Turn the radio on; you'll hear a friend. You will enjoy, you will learn, you will imagine, you will improve. Turn the radio on at home, in your car, in prison, on the beach, in a nursing home, you will not be alone; you will not be lonely. Newspapers fold, magazines come and go, television self-destructs, but radio remains the trusted common denominator in this nation.

Many of my friends have made the trip from St. Louis and New York to be here, and I appreciate their travel. My wife, Carole, and seven of my eight kids are here: Beverly, Jack, Chris, Bonnie, Dan, Betsy, Julie, all but Joe who announced the 49ers game today. I am proud of them and I know they are proud of me.

There is one aspect of our profession that I am not proud of and that is dirty radio. I wish that the owners, the general managers and the no-talent announcers who swim in the filth of dirty radio would go away. We don't want you, we certainly don't need you and I ask advertisers, please do not sponsor dirty radio. And, Mr. and Mrs. America, please don't listen.

After 47 years of broadcasting I wish I were just beginning. Thank you.

Citizen of the Year

(Text of Jack Buck's Citizen of the Year Acceptance Speech)

May 1, 2001
Missouri Athletic Club
St. Louis, Missouri

Mr. Hermann and Mr. Barksdale, thank you very much. Michael Pulitzer, Terry Egger, folks from the St. Louis Post Dispatch and Tracy Rouch who put this all together. Let's thank Tracy for all her fine work. I happily and humbly accept this award. The absence of Bill Maritz, who did so much for the community, saddens us all. Mike Eisenbath, thank you for the column that you wrote on the last day of the year when I got the good news that I was the one. Folks, this is not the Citizen of the Year, this is like *This is Your Life*. You met my wife, Carole, and I do this in the order that they are seated: My daughter, Julie; my daughter, Betsy; my daughter-in-law, Ann, with Natalie; Sarah, who belongs to Betsy; next in line is Christine with her husband, David; Beverly and Mike; my son Dan and his fiancée, Carrie; and Jack Buck, Jr. there are three Jack Bucks. Could that be it? Do I have any more kids? Oh, Joe Buck is with the ballclub in Florida and Bonnie Buck is in Chicago where she runs the internet news at NBC. Everybody has a brother-in-law: Joe and his wife, Pat.

Mary Lee and Bob Hermann hosted a party last night at their lovely home – it was wonderful. A few people got up and said some nice words about me. Duncan Bauman stood and said, "We have now touched the common man." Well, here I am, folks. There was another gentleman who stood up, I think it was Larry Roos, he said, "I voted against you, along with everybody at my table." And Larry, I spend a lot of time at your parking lot at Highway 170 and Eager Rd.

Folks, this is a wonderful night. And as I look around the room, I'm not going to name any names, but I see the world's greatest attorney, the world's greatest missionary, the world's second greatest attorney (you two fight it out), the world's greatest sportswriter (he's a Hall of Famer), the world's greatest jeweler, the world's greatest manager of baseball, the world's greatest baseball owner, the world's greatest chief of police, the world's greatest fire chief, the world's greatest manager of a Boys and Girls Club, the world's greatest marketing man, the world's greatest insurance man, the world's greatest travel agent. I'm telling you folks this is really like *This is Your Life.*

Mr. Hermann was correct when he was talking about the barber. The reason I usually talk in the chair is to keep the barber awake. He cut my hair today like he was looking for something.

They say you judge a man by the company he keeps. The former winners of this prestigious award are behind me (who probably can't see half of the audience because of these ears).

It boggles my mind how some people can vote for legalized gambling and to carry concealed weapons, but don't like the stadium idea. This new stadium is not going to happen this year or next; at best it's going to be five or six years from now. And let me say that, despite the mail I have been receiving, someday there will be a new stadium here in St. Louis. And I know about the other priorities in this area. I know about education. I know how good it is in the city and how good it isn't. One of my children, Beverly, recently won a state award, Teacher of the Year. I know a lot of the principals in these schools. I know that they need help. I know we can't shortchange these kids. I know we need new buildings. I know we just passed a bond issue for air conditioning in the schools, and that's wonderful. That's one of the groups in this area that we cannot desert. We have to care for those people who need our help. But I'll tell ya, if we ever lost this ball club in downtown St. Louis we're going to be hollering to the heavens to try to get other companies to come here. We'll give them all sorts of tax abatements to settle here in St. Louis and help build a tax base which is dwindling too rapidly. Why are people leaving? Because we're not doing things that we have to do to make downtown more attractive. Francis Slay, we're with you 100 percent. We'll do anything you ask us to do. I hope we'll get a new stadium here.

It may surprise you to hear me say that I belong up here today. But I do. Because I am a pinch hitter for the real Citizen of the Year. Who is it? I don't know. They don't know. We don't know. But I'll tell you who it could be. It could be a teacher who today took a little extra time to help a student. It could be a fireman who tonight will carry a child to safety. It could be a parent taking care of a child with MS, with muscular dystrophy, or cystic fibrosis. It could be a son or daughter caring for an aging, ailing parent. It could be a person donating a kidney to a sibling, donating money to the Backstoppers, or $40 million to the symphony. It could be a widow sending some of her social security money to the Salvation Army, or someone playing in the Salvation Army band. It could be a person still unable to move after being shot in the neck in Vietnam thirty-two years ago. It could be somebody packing sandbags to protect a river levee, somebody doing research at St. Louis U. or Washington U, a nurse staying overtime to administer a little extra tender loving care, a smiling nursing home worker, a police officer responding to anybody's call for help, someone who visits a prison and teaches the inmates how to read. Each of us in this room has done some of these things. I see people doing wonderful things with no thank-you, no recognition, and they keep doing it. We thank them today. We recognize them today. It's written in the program that I am a kind person. I hope I am. I try to be. I know what I have done. I know what I haven't done. But being a pinch hitter today makes me very happy—despite the tears. You know what? In the year 2001, I'm going to try to be Citizen of the Year. Thank you.

❋ ❋ ❋

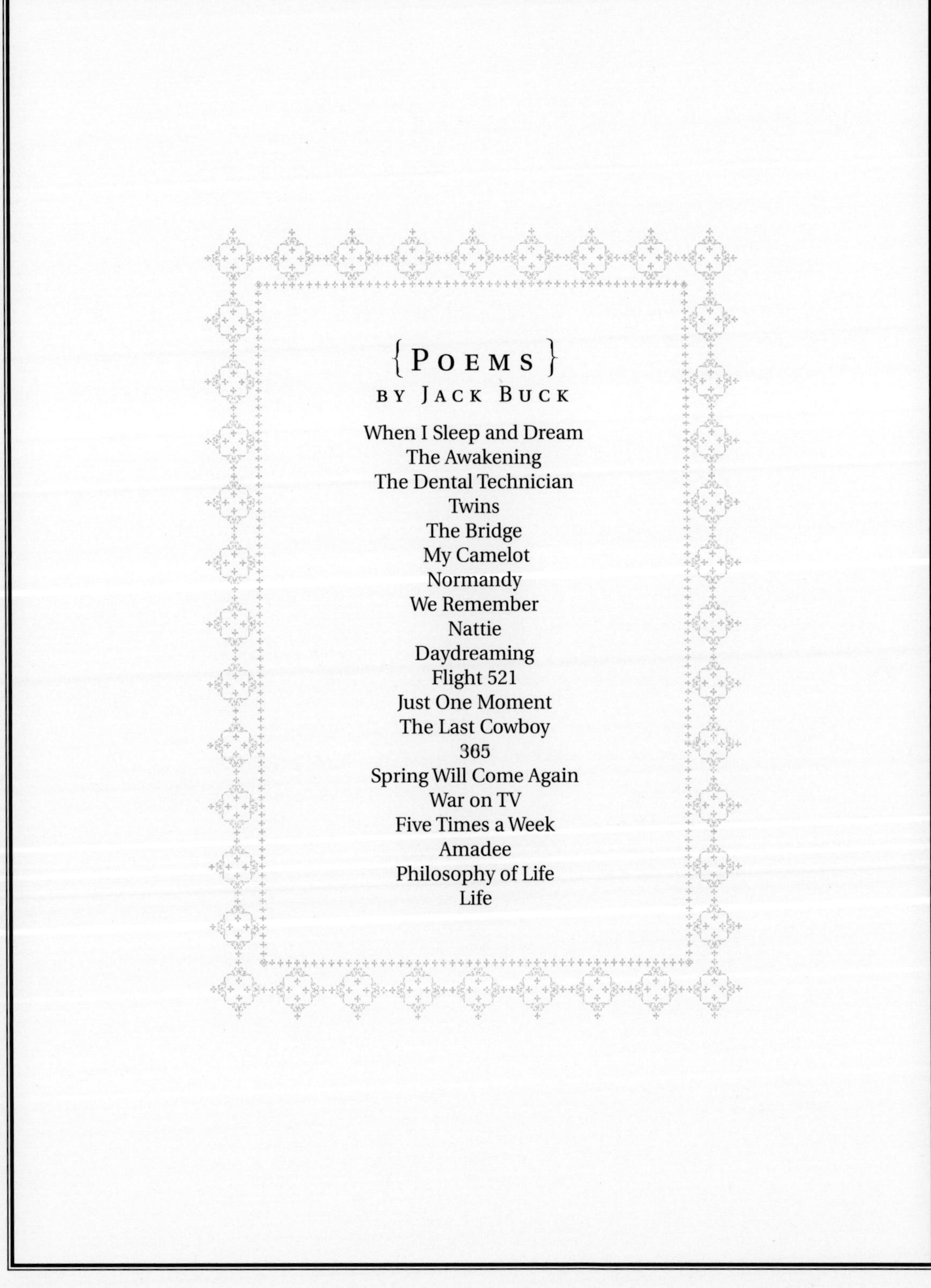

{Poems}

by Jack Buck

{ When I Sleep and Dream }

It's when I sleep and dream
that I have the most fun.
I'm Walter Mitty and Batman
rolled into one.

I can perform in mid-air
or star on the ice.
I can slam-dunk the ball
without thinking twice.

When I play in the Majors,
thanks to my sleep,
I flirt with .400
and I'm taking 'em deep.

I'm a kick-return guy
that everyone loves.
My opponents aren't happy
to put on the gloves.

I rescue pretty young girls
from an on rushing car.
I'm an astronaut too
and I know every star.

I solve math equations,
I star on the screen.
I'm the darnedest inventor
the world's ever seen.

I've traveled the world,
I make tough decisions.
I capture the bad boys
and put them in prisons.

Then my escapades end
when the sun wakes me up.
I spill half the coffee
I pour in my cup.

I leave the house
and trip on the hose.
I reach for the paper,
and I fall on my nose.

People all laugh
when I think I'm athletic.
When I swing a golf club
it's really pathetic.

I'm an ordinary guy
during the day.
I work hard for eight hours
and I pay my way.

I smile all the time
and folks don't know why.
It's because I'm daydreaming
about my pie in the sky.

I drive home, then I eat
and watch a little TV.
I jump into bed
to see who I will be.

{The Awakening} *for Rodney Stortz (September 25, 1997)*

You've had your plastic dinner
and you've watched the dumb TV.
The hospital halls are quiet,
you're as comfy as can be.

You tuck the pillow under
and you conjure up a dream.
It's lovely and exciting,
it's weird how real it seems.

You are coming to the best part,
it's the best dream you've ever had.
When suddenly the light explodes,
you think you've done
something bad.

The all-night nurse is
standing there,
she's bored – nothing to do.
She's seeking an activity
and decides to start with you.

She takes your blood pressure
for the fifteenth time that day.
And then she takes a specimen
she soon will throw away.

It's 4:30 in the morning,
a schedule you can't take.
She leaves to bother someone else,
and you lay there – wide awake!

{The Dental Technician}

She has lost that loving feeling.
Her tenderness has flown.
I would have canceled the
appointment if only I had known.

I've heard that there were people
who enjoy inflicting pain.
I've never heard of a dentist who
had no Novocain.

I'll save for her retirement.
I can't wait until that day.
She makes you squirm around
the chair.
And then they make you pay.

I'll get rid of all my teeth.
They're a pain in the neck to me.
Even my eyetooth is totally
unable to see.

I'll get even for the torture
That they have put me through.
I'll rush to see the dentist
The next time I have the flu.

Matt and Jack, Julie & Jeff's twins

{Twins}

(Written for a minister, September 1997)

One is sleeping,
one is not.
One is cold,
the other is hot.

One is nursing,
one is done.
Raising twins
is not much fun.

One needs a diaper,
the other is dry.
Things are changing,
so am I.

You can't count on
much help from me.
Just be glad
we didn't have three.

Hate to leave you
in such a lurch.
But it's time for me
to go to church!

My pal, Matt

{The Bridge}

Tortured young hearts
are sometimes mended.
But only when they
are lovingly tended.

Children will bend
when they're twisted and shoved.
But they will not break
when they know they are loved.

{My Camelot}

When I look back
at the things I've done,
the battles I've lost
and those I have won.

I settle on one word
that describes it all,
that word is FUN.
I've had a ball.

Helping to raise eight kids
of all shapes and sizes,
they've accomplished a lot
and created many surprises!

We've been blessed with good health,
our family has grown,
I've had my share of wealth,
I enjoy what I own.

I've seen much of the world,
I have traveled a lot,
and learned that my backyard
is my Camelot.

Most important right now,
before my life ends,
is to try to be kind
and earn some new friends.

Some say you can live again,
I don't know how that could be,
but if that is true,
I want to come back as me.

With the 9th Infantry Division
Germany, 1945

{Normandy}

(After a Visit to the Cemetery)

They chatter and laugh
as they pass by my grave
and that's the way it should be.

For what they have done
and what they will do
has nothing to do with me.

I was tossed ashore
by a friendly wave
with some unfriendly steel in
my head.

They chatter and laugh
as they pass by my grave
but I know they'll soon be dead.

They've counted more days
than I ever knew
and that's all right with me, too.

We're all souls in one pod,
all headed for God
too soon, or later, like you.

{We Remember}

It's Memorial Day. Some are still asking why.
Close your eyes and remember as the colors pass by.
Which war was yours? How long did it last?
Whose face do you see when the flag's at half-mast?

Who marched away and didn't return?
For whom did you pray? For whom do you yearn?

Dog tags and telegrams
A knock on the door
Were you the parents they were looking for?
The pain never leaves, it has impacted us all,
When a family is left with a name carved in a wall.

They fought and they fell, unaware of their glory,
We must remember them always and continue their story.

Appreciate where you live, enjoy living free.
Many flowers never blossomed, they died…
For you and for me.

Natalie, Ann and Joe's daughter

{Nattie}

Ann and Joe's daughter

She's a sweet little girl
who's now almost two.
She learns every day
new things she can do.

She says, "daddy" and "mommy"
and "peez" and "bye-bye."
With a smile that's as wide
as the western sky.

Her eyes sparkle and dance
when a new thought hits her brain.
And she now knows the difference
between a bird and a plane.

She gives leaves as gifts
and points and yells at the moon.
And we already know
she'll grow up too soon.

A dog is a "roo-roo,"
a duck is a "guck."
That's the vocabulary
of Natalie Buck.

Things change for the better
when she comes into view.
She's a prayer that's been answered,
a wish that's come true.

Love, Dee Dee (That's what she calls me)

{Daydreaming}

(Written 1976)

I don't know exactly what it is,
it's almost always been that way.
No matter where I am or who
  I'm with,
I know exactly what to say.

Other times I draw a blank
and take on a certain air.
Disinterested or ill-equipped,
I find I just don't care.

When I feel good, elevated just right,
and then those around me don't.
I should adjust, be as they are,
I try to, I'd like to, but I won't.

After all my years I've concluded,
that those around me could be
  included.
Know my thoughts, my moods,
  my feelings,
but to let them in would just
  be stealing.

So until there is nothing there,
I'll exist with a particular air.
It could have helped or hurt if they
  had known,
but they, like I, are on their own.

Jack's home March 1942 - June 1943: A Great Lakes Iron Ore Carrier

{Flight 521}

When traveling across the States
by plane,
One thing is sadly clear.
Not many kids use the
baseball fields,
No matter the time of year.

There was a time many years ago,
When every boy played the game
every day.
From morning 'til dark,
In the street or a park,
A ball was always coming
your way.

It was Indian Ball or Nine on
a Side,
Or a Hot Box – we called it a Pickle.
You played 'til you dropped,
You just never stopped,
Back then you bought a ball for
a nickel.

As we grew through the years,
Some starred and drew cheers.
But most learned they would play
just for fun.
You knew where you stood with
that round piece of wood,
Would you ever hit that Dramatic
Home Run?

It was hard but you did it,
Tough to catch,
Tough to hit it.

The challenge was
constantly there,
And the knowledge you took
wasn't found in a book,
It was in the grass, and the dirt
and fresh air.

You played where you were told,
By your pals who were old.
You declared yourself safe or out.
Take care what you said,
You could get hit in the head,
And watch a game turn into
a bout.

You learned not to cheat,
Handle pressure and heat,
And always try to be fair.

What a shame to look down,
At every city and town,
All those diamonds and
nobody there.

Busch Stadium

{Just One Moment}

(San Diego, 1998)

I saw a kid in a wheelchair today,
and he deeply affected me.
He was on the field at a baseball game,
and was a gut-wrenching sight to see.

I would guess his age at 11 or so,
his body was twisted and bent.
Palsy has clutched him since the day he
was born,
and dictated the life he has spent.

His mother and father were there with him,
this was not the dream she had dreamed.
They watched the players hit, run and throw,
and weren't jealous, or so it seemed.

I looked at the grass, the sun and the sky,
and pondered the beauties of earth.
And wondered how often he asks why,
and what he thinks life is worth?

This little guy couldn't walk or talk,
when he shook his head "no" it meant "yes."
How much he knew of what others
go through
is anybody's guess.

His dad held him up so he could see
a slugger hit one a mile.
Then a hero gave him an autographed ball
and all he could do was smile.

{The Last Cowboy}

(Written for Gene Autry's 83rd Birthday Party, 1990)

As America grew
and headed west,
Gene Autry was there
and he was the best.

He tapped telegraph keys
then starred on the screen,
the greatest Saturday star
young eyes had seen.

He wore a white hat
and the kids always knew
he'd do the right thing
they wanted him to.

He could shoot at a target
and invariably hit it
while jumping a river,
and he sang as he did it.

He crooned "South of the Border"
and sang on Christmas morn,
the most glamorous cowboy
ever born.

His ride through life
is matched by no other,
a business tycoon,
yet everyone's brother.

He has enjoyed life to the fullest
and made our lives richer,
but he'd have traded it all
for a World Series pitcher.

We salute him today
and we'll love him tomorrow,
the last cowboy's life
was ours to borrow.

Little did he know
when he named his horse,
he was describing himself –
Champion, of course!

{365}

When someone asks you
your favorite sport,
you answer, "Baseball" in a blink.

There are certain qualities
you must possess
and you're more attached than
you think.

In the frozen grip of winter,
I'm sure you'll agree with me.
Not a day goes by
without someone
talking baseball to some degree.

The calendar flips on
New Year's Day,
the Super Bowl comes and it goes.
Get the other sports out of
the way,
the green grass and
the fever grows.

It's time to pack a bag
and take a trip
to Arizona or the Sunshine State.

Perhaps you can't go,
but there's the radio,
so you listen, you root and
you wait.

They start the campaign,
pomp and pageantry reign,
you claim the pennant
on opening day.

From April 'til fall
you follow the bouncing
white ball,
your team is set to go all the way.

They fall short of the Series,
you have a case of the wearies
and need a break from the game.

But when Christmas bells jingle
you feel the same tingle
and you're ready for more of
the same.

It will be hot dogs for dinner,
six months of heaven a winner,
Yes, baseball has always been it.

You would amaze all your friends
if they knew to what ends
you'd go for a little old hit.

The best times you've had
have been with your mom and
your dad
and a bat and a ball and a glove.

From the first time you played
'til the last time you prayed
it's been a simple matter of love.

{Spring Will Come Again}

(Written September 23, 1997)

There is a sadness that you feel in September
of the year.
When your baseball team is out of the race and
there's nothing left to cheer.
The weather doesn't help, it's chilly and
it's raining.
And you let go of the dreams you dreamed
when your team was in spring training.

The stands are almost empty, there's no
reason to come around.
And the stadium seems hollow, an echo
punctuates each sound.
You can hear the umpire call the pitches,
hear the coach when he claps his hands.
There is no rhythmic stomping,
no wave sweeps through the stands.

It's strange how cruel the game can be.
Despite the love you give it,
You talk baseball every day
You nurture it – you live it.

They're playing out the schedule, no one
seems to care.
But a baseball fan's life will begin anew the
next time spring is in the air.

{ War on TV }

(Written September, 1997)

I see TV commercials
for the Army everyday.
They're swooping down
  in choppers,
Taking everything in
  their way.

The food is good,
  the money's fine,
You'll always be on
  the attack.
The one thing they don't
  tell you
Is that someone will be
  shooting back!

{ Five Times a Week }

(Written September 26, 1997)

It really is a challenge
to drive to work and back.
You meet every crazy driver,
every kook and maniac.

They hang their arm out the window
as their cars go in and out.
And they wave at you as they go by
with a finger sticking out!

They are certain that the limit
is just a bunch of bunk.
They're always right behind you
with their bumper in your trunk!

They're smoking and they're phoning,
if they have a hangnail they will file it.
They don't care about other folks,
their car's on automatic pilot.

Their radio is always loud,
the music must be good.
They couldn't hear an airplane
if it landed on their hood!

But the busiest drivers are the girls
with their lipstick and their comb.
I think I'll sell my vehicle
and earn my living from my home!

{ Amadee }

(Amadee Wohlschlaeger was one of the greatest sports cartoonists!)

How many in the room tonight have been assaulted by Amadee's cigar?
Had to hold your nose?
Get rid of your clothes?
And have the upholstery cleaned in your car.

How many here in the room tonight
Have made the biggest mistake of your life?
Almost met your end – tried to out drink our friend
And had to be carried home to your wife.

We shall forgive those slight indiscretions as we honor
Wohlschlaeger tonight.
We'll have one of those memorable sessions.
It's overdue – but we'll make it right.
We have gathered together to show our admiration for this talented man.
His work stands apart – a unique form of art
Only he can do what he can.

When his clock chimes again, he'll be 90 years old.
Not many were there when he started.
How many cartoons? Only heaven knows
For most of his friends have departed.

The Weatherbird was his creation.
The forecast always changed the bird's look.
But sports cartoons spread his name through the nation.
He was the best in everyone's book.

He covered sports for 53 years.
Developed numerous quirks.
They gave him a watch when he called it quits.
Later – they gave him the works.

With thunderous laugh and a ready smile,
He still gets around everyday.
Likes to golf – loves to fish – he'll let you set the style.
Will always drink to your health – IF YOU PAY!

He wears a battered old hat.
At night he prowls like a cat.
He knows every bartender in town.
He has seen the sun rise
More than most other guys.
He's a man you just can't keep down.

It was a great idea to do what we've done
To display his fantastic collection.
Soon it will go for another show
in Cooperstown's Hall of Fame direction.

Let's declare a toast to our honoree
And continue our evening of fun.
Herr Wohlschlaeger – now –
please stand – take a bow.
You certainly are – Number One!!!

Portrait of Jack Buck, drawn by Amadee Wohlschlaeger.

{Philosophy of Life}

Though there are many laughs
and tons and tons of strife,
I've been able to minimize it
and state my philosophy of life.

Simply put – you choose a road,
the one you'll travel on,
You go and go and go and go
and pretty soon you're gone.

{Life}

It's nice to know
When the day is done
That you've done your work,
And had some fun.

You've hurt no one and
You've helped some others
because you know we're
sisters and brothers.

The nicest thought: If the
Lord lets us borrow, is that
you can hop out of bed and do
the same thing tomorrow.

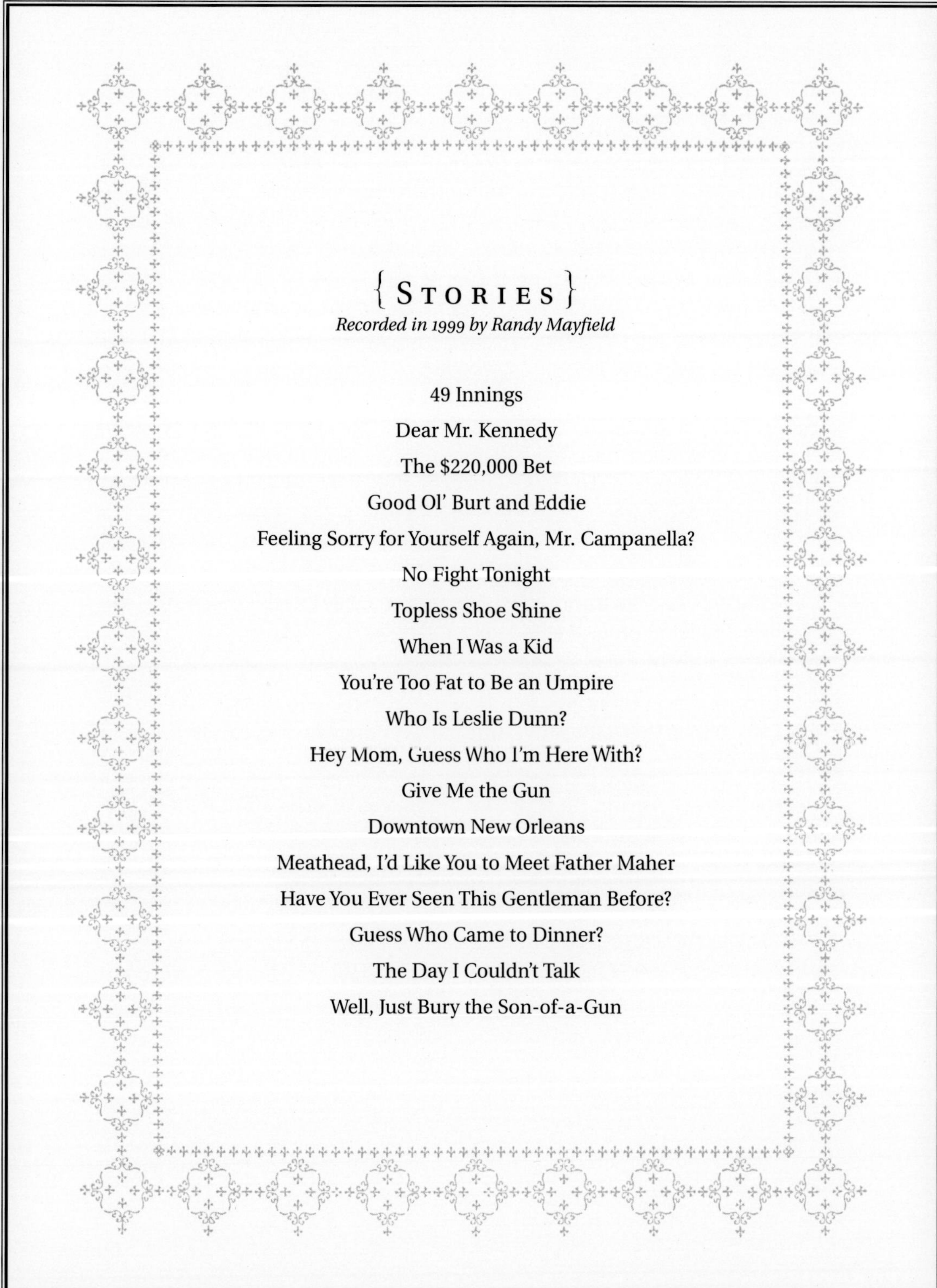

{ Stories }

Recorded in 1999 by Randy Mayfield

49 Innings

Dear Mr. Kennedy

The $220,000 Bet

Good Ol' Burt and Eddie

Feeling Sorry for Yourself Again, Mr. Campanella?

No Fight Tonight

Topless Shoe Shine

When I Was a Kid

You're Too Fat to Be an Umpire

Who Is Leslie Dunn?

Hey Mom, Guess Who I'm Here With?

Give Me the Gun

Downtown New Orleans

Meathead, I'd Like You to Meet Father Maher

Have You Ever Seen This Gentleman Before?

Guess Who Came to Dinner?

The Day I Couldn't Talk

Well, Just Bury the Son-of-a-Gun

In 1950, I was broadcasting in Columbus for the Redbirds and we were playing the Minneapolis Millers. Rollie Helmsley (a former Major League catcher) was our manager. We had an outfielder by the name of Larry Miggins. He was a very religious person, and he had ten kids. He was playing left field when a ball was hit into the seats and bounced back to the field. Miggins caught the ball and threw it back to the infield. It was called a double and there was a big argument. Finally the home plate umpire (I even remember his name, Bill Jackowski, who later came up to the big leagues) left home plate to ask the outfielder if he had really caught the ball. Can you imagine that? There was no instant replay back then; there was barely radio. We had just graduated from the megaphone. The umpire walked all the way out there and Helmsley said, "If he tells him, I'll kill that son of a _____." And the next thing you know, the umpire was signaling the home run from left field. Miggins told him it was a home run and we lost the game. Miggins wasn't in very good standing in Columbus. But we won what they called the Little World Series at that time in 1950, so it all turned out well. Honesty is the best policy, but sometimes it could get you killed.

Ellis "Cot" Deal was a pitcher in Columbus, Ohio. It was a 23-inning game and we were going to give away an automobile at the end of the game. Deal pitched all 23 innings and drove in the winning run in the 23rd inning.

In about the 15th inning a player by the name of Les Fusselman was rounding third base. He was going to score the winning run and he lost a shoe. His shoe came off and he stopped to pick it up! He was thrown out at home and we went on to play 23 innings.

One of the fans died of a heart attack during the course of the game, and the fellow who won the car was 80 years old and had never driven a car in his life.

I got home at about three o'clock in the morning and my wife said, "Why so late? Where have you been?"

I said, "Just another night at the ballpark."

Dear Mr. Kennedy

A few years ago I was in Philadelphia with the Cardinals. I was going to play golf the next day and I had a pain in my back so I said something to the trainer. The trainer gave me some Feldene, which, I have come to learn, is a rather treacherous pain drug. A lot of people take it for arthritis, but for some people it may cause serious damage to the stomach. The trainer said, "Here take this, you'll feel better."

The pain wasn't really that bad, but I took the pill anyway.

The next morning I started passing blood. One of my kids was working in the East and we were going to have lunch together, so I had to persevere during the course of the day. I knew I was sick, so I called and made an airline reservation to go home. I wanted to go home. When everybody left for the ballpark, I went to the airport. I was about to get on the plane in Philadelphia to return to St. Louis when there was a blip in the radar and the entire East Coast was shut down with regard to air traffic. I couldn't get on the plane.

There was a gentleman by the name of Kennedy who was a skycap. He happened to be a black man. Black people have a lot of Irish names: Kennedy, Doyle and so forth. Anyway, he took care of me as no stranger ever has. TWA didn't have a lounge, so he took me over to the United Airlines lounge and we waited for the radar to be fixed so the plane could depart. When my flight was canceled he put me in a cab and I went back to the ballpark. By that time I had lost about four pints of blood. They put me on the floor of the clubhouse, brought in the doctor, called an ambulance and wheeled me off to the hospital. I had a bleeding ulcer. If I had gotten on that airplane I would have died. There is no doubt.

I wonder who caused the radar to shut down that day. I think I know.

The $220,000 Bet

Amarillo Slim was a professional gambler (a poker player) in 1975. Man, was it that long ago? I went out to Las Vegas to film the World Series of Poker for NBC. I've had a good life, haven't I?

I was acquainted with Amarillo Slim and he was in the Hold 'Em tournament. There were 22 players who put up $10,000 each; winner take all, one winner, $220,000.

I was doing the telecast and before the tournament started I said, "Slim, if you get knocked out of the tournament will you do the color with me on the telecast?"

He said, "Yeah, but you'd better get somebody else 'cause I'm gonna win this thing. I won't be available."

In the first round he was playing head-to-head with a guy who made a small bet. Slim pushed in all $10,000 and raised him. The guy looked at him for about a minute and said, "I'll call you. What have you got?"

Slim said, "A pair of jacks."

The guy said, "I've got aces."

Amarillo Slim turned and said, "Hey Jack, wait a minute. What are you paying for that job?"

He got knocked out in the first round.

Young Jack Binion was a friend of mine. His father owned Binion's Horseshoe Casino in downtown Las Vegas. Binion's has a million dollars cash in the lobby and they'll book any bet on the crap table. You show them you have the money and you can bet a million dollars – five million, ten million – whatever you want to bet on any roll of the dice.

Jack Binion Jr. was in the poker tournament with a fellow by the name of Doyle Brunson. Brunson was one of the last two remaining players. The other player was an automobile dealer from Houston.

All the money was in the middle of the table and Brunson said to his opponent, "What do you have?"

And he said, "Aces up."

There was one more card to turn and Brunson said, "You've got me, I've got tens and deuces."

They turned the other card up, I can still see it: ten of clubs, full house, $220,000.

Then I had a drink with Brunson and Binion. They were players in the tournament. Binion said, "Man, we needed that money. We played golf the other day and this dodo missed a putt for $90,000." That's the way they gamble when they play golf out there. Talk about a different world. One round of golf, $90,000 riding on a putt. I would have missed it, also!

Good Ol' Burt and Eddie

I announced the first games of the American Football League in 1960, and I was usually on the West Coast working with a fellow by the name of George Ratterman who had been a quarterback at Notre Dame and we stayed at Gene Autry's Continental Hotel on Sunset Boulevard in Los Angeles.

One Sunday morning I was having breakfast with my director, Andy Sedaris, who did many Olympic directing jobs. Burt Reynolds came swinging down the street. He sat down and joined us. I bought breakfast for him because he didn't have a nickel in his pocket. He had just come from college and had gone to the coast to try to make it in the movies; and as we all know, he made it big.

In 1990 I was doing a TV baseball Game of the Week in Milwaukee when I saw Burt Reynolds again. I introduced myself to him and he had no idea who I was. He didn't want to know who I was and didn't pay any attention. I'll never buy him breakfast again.

That reminds me. You know that movie star, Eddie Murphy? I was doing a boxing match in Atlantic City, New Jersey. I was working with "Boom Boom" Mancini. I was sitting at ringside, wearing a tuxedo, and, you know, you would have to be an idiot not to know I was officially involved in the telecast of that fight. Eddie Murphy came in with his entourage; he must have had about 20 people around him. He had ringside seats. I walked over, introduced myself, stuck my hand out to him and he looked at me like I was a cloud. He never moved, he didn't shake my hand and he didn't say hello. I turned around and went back to my announcing position.

I was doing a record show in those days at KMOX. It was a morning show and I was on the air from 9 a.m. to noon. After I returned home, I was doing my show and there was a new record on the market by Eddie Murphy of all people. I introduced the record and I started to play it, then I stopped it right in the middle and I said, "To hell with him."

I got even with him. He didn't know it, but I got even. I took the record off and I said on the air that he was the most impolite person I had ever met. You should have heard the phones ring. Some people agreed with me and other people disagreed with me, but that's the way I felt about him.

Back to "Boom Boom" Mancini, We televised fights in Atlantic City which were sponsored by Budweiser. I came home from a trip and asked Joe Buck if he had seen the fight. He said, "Yeah, did you hear what 'Boom Boom' said? He cursed on the air." I said, "I didn't hear him swear." He said, "Play the tape."

I happened to have the tape with me. I was talking about one of the fighters. I said, "There's no doubt that he's behind on points in the fight, but he's not finished. If he rallies a little bit, he's still got a chance to win."

And just as clear as a bell, something I didn't hear when I was seated right along side him, Mancini said, "Yeah, if he gets his shit together he's gonna be OK."

Joe heard that on the air. In the midst of doing the broadcast of the fight, I never even heard it.

Feeling Sorry for Yourself Again, Mr. Campanella?

I got to know Roy Campanella rather well, as did a lot of people, when he was working for the Dodgers after the accident that paralyzed him. He was at the height of his career when he was involved in an automobile accident and was paralyzed. Subsequently, he was inducted into the Hall of Fame the same day as Stan Musial.

Campanella told me this story during the course of an interview. He was in his hospital bed shortly after the accident. He had gone from being a Major League catcher to a person who was paralyzed from the neck down. There was a little kid in the hospital – maybe 12 years old – who had no arms or legs. He wore a leather body stocking and he used to roll down the halls of the hospital a mile a minute. He would wheel in and out of hospital rooms spreading joy wherever he went.

Campanella was sitting in bed one day with tears rolling down his cheeks when the kid rolled into his room, looked up at him and said, "Feeling sorry for yourself, Mr. Campanella?" and turned and rolled out of the room. Roy told me that the youngster's remark did more to help his rehabilitation than anything else.

No Fight Tonight

There was another time I was broadcasting a fight and Carole was with me in Atlantic City. We were just about to go on the air. Carole was across the ring from me and she was visiting with a lady seated next to her.

Carole started waving her hands at me and I was irritated that she would interrupt the beginning of the telecast. She was shaking her head "no." I finally took off my headset and ran around to the other side of the ring and she said, "Calvin Grove is not fighting tonight."

I said, "What do you mean, he's not fighting? He's gonna come out here in a couple of minutes."

She said, "This is his mother and she told me that Calvin is sick and he's not boxing tonight."

I ran back, put my headset on, and what do you know, I heard "Ladies and gentlemen, Calvin Grove will not appear this evening."

The crowd started throwing stuff around the auditorium. A substitute fighter needed to be found and we had to fill the time because Calvin Grove didn't answer the bell – Carole knew it before I did. I interviewed Rocky Graziano, the former great middleweight champion, to kill the time. That interview was probably better than the fight would have been, anyhow.

"Topless Shoe Shine, Upstairs, $5"

I was in San Francisco with the late Bill McPhail and Pat Summerall. Bill was my boss at CBS and Pat Sommerall and I used to work together on TV. In fact, we did a Super Bowl together when I was doing the play-by-play and he was doing the color. He now does the play-by-play with John Madden.

We were out one night and it really was one of the most fun nights of my life. We were drinking a little beer and kicking around in the nightclub district up on Broadway in San Francisco. We ended up playing topless ping-pong – doubles – Pat and I against two girls (that's two against four, I think).

We really had a lot of laughs; we always did. later we were walking down the street and there was a sign that said, "Topless Shoe Shine, Upstairs, $5." So I paid our $5 to the guy downstairs and went upstairs to find another fellow shining shoes with his shirt off – topless! They got the money first, and they ripped off the city slickers.

When I Was a Kid...

When we were kids, my friends and I used to swim in the Connecticut River. I lived in Holyoke, Massachusetts. People tell me you can't swim in the Connecticut River now because of the pollution, but it used to be quite nice. Some of the older kids used to swim across the river to Mt. Holyoke College, a girls' school. I guess I was too young to realize why they were doing it.

That reminds me of a story Mike Roarty tells where one kid says to the other, "How old are you?" And that kid says, "Seven. How old are you?" And the first kid answers, "I don't know." So the other kid asks, "Do you like girls?" And he says, "No." Then he says, "Well, you're six."

Anyway, we used to swim in the river. We would enter the caves below the water level, dig up dinosaur tracks out of the shale. We'd bring them up, show them to the other guys, throw them away and go home. You know the Sinclair Oil logo with the dinosaur? By the time they started buying those dinosaur tracks, they couldn't find many. I think we wiped out the dinosaur tracks from the Connecticut River.

You're Too Fat to Be an Umpire

This is a story about Bruce Froemming. A short little fat guy, a National League umpire, a very good friend and a very good umpire.

Jay Randolph and I flew into San Francisco and I got the luggage while Randolph went to get the rental car. I was standing there with the luggage when Bruce Froemming came by with a rental car. He was going to pick up his buddies who had gone to get their luggage. Jay and I got to Candlestick Park before the umpires did. The young fellow at the gate waved us down and we identified ourselves and he let us in. I talked to the kid and told him what I wanted him to do. I told him that Bruce Froemming would be coming along; he was in a Lincoln Town Car and wearing an ABC-TV cap. I told the kid what to do so when Froemming and the other umpires arrived. He wouldn't let them in the gate.

He waved them down and Froemming, who was a very bombastic sort, said, "Hey, let us in, we're the umpires."

He looked at Froemming and said, "You can't be an umpire. You're not an umpire."

Froemming asked, "Why not?"

And the kid said, "You're too fat to be an umpire."

Froemming jumped out of the car and grabbed the kid by the throat and started shaking him and the kid said, "Jack Buck gave me $20 to say that to you."

The next time Froemming saw me he grabbed me around the neck.

Later, he came to St. Louis and he was at Charlie Gitto's having a meal one night after a ballgame. He met a well-known priest here in town by the name of Slattery. He introduced himself to the priest and said, "I'm Bruce Froemming, a National League umpire."

And Father Slattery said, "You can't be an umpire."

And he asked, "Why not?"

Father Slattery said, "You're too fat to be an umpire."

I had told the story on the air and the people had heard it so we burned him twice.

Who Is Leslie Dunn?

It was a really busy time. I was doing football and baseball, working at KMOX, traveling here and there and emceeing banquets. I emceed a luncheon during a baseball meeting in Dallas, then I had to emcee a dinner for CBS Radio that night.

We had a new boss at CBS whom I hadn't met; his name was Bob Hoskins. After the banquet was over – you always know if it went well or not, and it had gone very well – Bob Hoskins came over to me and said, "Nicely done." I thought he was introducing himself and I thought he said, "Leslie Dunn." So for the rest of the evening I introduced the new boss at CBS Radio as Leslie Dunn.

That night when I finally realized that wasn't his name, I said to Carole, "Guess what I did?" And I told her the story of how I introduced Bob Hoskins as Leslie Dunn to about 40 people that night. I finally had to call him in New York to clear my conscience. He hadn't paid any attention to it but it caused me a lot of anguish.

Hey Mom, Guess Who I'm Here With?

I was at the LaScala Restaurant in New York having dinner with Red Schoendienst and Stan Musial. The LaScala Restaurant was right next to Jimmy Ryan's, a Dixieland place. Across the street was Eddie Condon's place, where Dizzie Gillespie used to play. We met Bobby Scott, the songwriter and performer who wrote "He Ain't Heavy, He's My Brother." Bobby Scott was smitten with meeting Musial and Schoendienst. He had been drinking and he pulled up a chair and sat down with us and proceeded to get even more drunk. After dinner we went across the street to Eddie Condon's place and he went to the telephone and called his mother and he was going to put Musial on the phone. He said, "Mom, guess who I'm here with? I'm here with f---ing Stan Musial." Can you imagine that? He put Stanley on the phone and Stanley talked to this guy's mother, but I couldn't get over that. He was using the "F" word to his mother. To this day I can always get a rise out of Stan by reminding him of that story.

Bobby Scott said, "If there's any trouble in this place you guys don't have to worry about a thing." And he pulled out a .38 automatic and put it on the table in the nightclub.

I was the first one to speak. I said, "I'll see you guys at the ballpark tomorrow." And out we went – without Bobby Scott.

"Give Me the Gun"

I was at Camp Stewart Georgia in 1943 and in downtown Savannah a soldier and a cab driver got into a dispute, and the cab driver pulled a gun. There was a bunch of GI's downtown and all the cab drivers gathered around. It was an ugly situation, but everybody was staying away from that gun except one GI. He was a blond-haired GI. He walked from across the street to the other sidewalk and came face-to-face with the guy with the gun. He reached out and said, "Give me the gun." The cab driver gave it to him and all hell broke loose. It was one of the biggest fights I've ever seen in my life! I can still see that soldier walking across the street with the gun aimed right at his belly.

Downtown New Orleans

Downtown New Orleans is like many major cities in this country. You can get in trouble in a big hurry if you go off the beaten path. The French Quarter is a well-known part of the city with a lot of entertainment. If you get outside the perimeter of that French Quarter, you can get mugged just as easily in New Orleans as you can in any other city.

A lot of tourists go to visit the cemeteries in New Orleans to see the grave sites of the pirates and so forth. The grave sites are usually tombs because of the high water level. They can't bury people below the ground, so they are put in tombs. Criminals often target these tourists.

My wife and I were walking down the street in New Orleans. It was Super Bowl time. I saw two guys squaring off, one of them was a sailor and the other was a civilian. They were inching closer and closer. I said to Carole, "Let's get down about a half a block away from this and then we'll watch what happens." About that time some guy flew over the hood of a car and landed on top of the sailor and another fight broke out. That should have been on film. I mean it was one of the best ever.

"Meathead, I'd Like You to Meet Father Maher."

There was a priest at Saint Louis University by the name of Trafford Maher, who was in charge of the Theology Department. He was a wonderful gentleman – one of the most intelligent people I have ever met – and I ended up on an airplane with him one winter night.

I was going to a boxing match at the old Madison Square Garden in New York City. ABC was televising the match and some friends of mine were doing the telecast. As we were landing in New York I asked the priest, "Father, would you like to go to the fights with me?" He said, "No, I've got to give a speech in the morning. I've got to work on it tonight. I can't afford to go." I said, "Well, you would really like it. Emile Griffith is fighting a fellow by the name of Hernandez." Griffith later became a middleweight champion. He was a very good fighter. We were getting off the airplane and the priest tapped me on the shoulder and said, "Jack, I'm going with you." I said, "Oh, wonderful."

We took a cab downtown to the old Madison Square Garden. The TV truck was parked outside and that TV truck was nothing like you see today. It was actually a bakery truck that had been transformed into a television truck. It was a cold, windy night and I opened the door to the truck and pushed the priest in ahead of me.

Hugh Beach – we called him "meathead" – was the director. Just as I pushed the priest into the truck – wouldn't you know it – he started to swear at the switcher, one of the technicians. I was tapping him on the shoulder and the swear words were one after the other with this priest standing there. Finally, I said, "Meathead, I'd like you to meet Father Maher." Meathead was wearing an overcoat, that's how cold it was in the television truck. We're talking about ancient times here. Without missing a beat he reached into his pocket and pulled out an apple and said, "Here Father, have an apple." And he turned around and started to swear at the guy again.

Well, I hustled him out of there and we ended up at ringside. It was a heck of a fight and the blood started to fly. This priest was getting blood all over him, I'm sure for the first time in his life, because he was a very gentle person. I took the priest into the dressing room after the fight and introduced him to Emile Griffith, who was covered with perspiration after his victory, and he rushed over and gave the priest a great big hug and invited him to a party at the Roosevelt Hotel, which we had to decline.

Outside on the sidewalk Father Maher said to me, "Jack, this has been one of the greatest evenings of my life. Do me a favor? Never invite me to go with you again."

"Have You Ever Seen This Gentleman Before?"

As I was leaving an afternoon ballgame in St. Petersburg, a fellow walked up to me and said, "John Buck?"

I said, "Yes, sir." And he handed me a subpoena. He was a federal marshal and I was to report to the court in Chicago. I called the court and talked to the judge. The judge said that as long as he knew where I was going to be each day, I didn't have to go to Chicago until he called.

I was in Los Angeles and an FBI agent asked me to meet him in the hotel lobby. I had no idea what all this was about. He showed me a picture of a fellow in a soft hat, and he asked, "Have you ever seen this gentleman before?"

I said, "Not that I know of."

He said, "Well, if you've never seen him, you never will because he has disappeared."

Later I got a phone call that I had to go to Chicago to testify, and I still had no idea what any of this was all about.

In Chicago, I went to the Hyatt Hotel and checked into my room. Then I got another room, checked into that room and slept there because I didn't know who was after whom or what was going on.

I went to court the next day. The FBI asked me to look through a window into the courtroom to see if I knew any of the people at the defense table. There was a defense attorney sitting there with a blond lady. The FBI people asked, "Do you know any of the people you see there?" And I said, "No." I ended up on the witness stand with the same question, "Did I know anybody in the courtroom?" And I told them that aside from the FBI people, I didn't recognize anybody.

Then the defense attorney asked, "Were you in Los Angeles on such and such a date?"

"Yes."

"What were you there for?"

"I was there to do a Bears/Rams football game."

He asked, "Isn't it true that that game was played on a Sunday afternoon and not on a Saturday night?"

I answered, "Yes, because of the Watts riots, they changed the game from Saturday night to Sunday afternoon."

And he asked, "What were the dates of the Watts riots?"

I said, "I don't know, sir. I could go to the library and look it up for you."

The judge hit the desk with his gavel. It sounded like a cannon and he said, "You'll save your wise remarks for the airwaves, Mr. Buck."

The interrogation of me was fruitless and when I got off the stand the FBI agent said, "Did you see that blond at the table?"

"Yes I did."

"She was in the bar at the Continental Hotel on Sunset Boulevard. You did the football game on Sunday afternoon, went back to your hotel and went into the bar. The fellow whose picture we showed you earlier, who has now disappeared, offered to buy you a drink. You turned him down and went to your room.

I said, "I did?"

He said, "That's right. If you had recognized that blonde, she was meeting the guy with the hat. He had come from Chicago. She was there from San Francisco and there were some stolen securities that she had given to him. He took them to New York and they built a building with those stolen securities. If you had said you saw her in the bar that night, we would have made our case."

So that's how you can get into trouble. I didn't even accept the drink.

During the Bears/Rams game that Sunday afternoon, the Bears went the length of the field and had first and goal when a kid ran out onto the field. He was a pretty big kid, he looked to be about 16 or 17 years old, and they had to halt play.

The police were chasing him. The ushers were chasing him. Nobody could catch him. Soon the people in the stands were rooting for this kid to get away, but he made a mistake. He got too close to where the Bears were and he had interrupted their touchdown drive. Mike Ditka, who was playing tight end at that time for the Bears, stepped out and hit this kid with a forearm underneath the chin while he was running at full speed. He was thrown about 20 feet in the air and he slammed to the ground. I thought Ditka was going to start another riot; the people were booing him.

To this day, I tease Ditka – who is in the Hall of Fame – about hitting that kid, and he says, "Jack, if you were a businessman and somebody came in and stood on your desk, what would you do? That's what I did." By the way, they arrested the kid, took him to court and the judge looked at him and said, "You won't do that again, will you? Case dismissed."

Guess Who Came to Dinner?

Before I started broadcasting in Columbus I was going to Ohio State and working at a gas station. I frequently worked from eleven at night 'til seven in the morning. There was a fellow – a pilot for American Airlines – who came to the station with an old Packard automobile; it was in mint condition. Whenever he came in he would tell me about the trips that he was taking. He usually flew the route from Columbus to Boston. This went on for a couple of months and he and I got to be quite friendly.

In addition to working in the gas station I worked in a restaurant at noon for my lunches. I was in that restaurant one day for lunch and the Wiedemann Beer truck made a delivery. Can you guess who walked in with a keg of beer on his shoulder? It was the airline pilot; he wasn't an airline pilot. He was a deliveryman and he had been b---s---ing me all this time. Well, he looked at me, and I looked at him, and not a word was said, but he knew the jig was up.

Time marched on. I started broadcasting baseball in Columbus. There was a fan there named Virginia Acton. She was always inviting my wife and me to come to dinner at her folks' house. I had turned her down so often that I finally had to agree that we would go to their house one night for dinner, and we did. She told us as we were seated that her boyfriend was running a little late but he was coming. There was a knock at the door, and when the door was opened, guess who was standing there! It was the airline pilot/beer truck deliveryman who was Virginia Acton's boyfriend. He sat at the table across from me. Dinner lasted two hours. He never said one word during the entire evening. He was afraid I was going to blow the whistle on him and tell everyone what a b---s---er he was. That was an awkward night for him and me.

The Day I Couldn't Talk

In 1969 Roy Campanella was inducted into the Hall of Fame at Cooperstown the same day as Stan Musial. Bob Burns, Harry Caray and I were broadcasting for KMOX and we had a good time of it as Musial was introduced. When they brought Roy Campanella to the stage in a wheelchair, Harry Caray handed the microphone to me because he couldn't talk. I handed it to Bob Burns because I couldn't talk, and Burns handed it back to Harry Caray because *he* couldn't talk. What a moment that was!

"Well, Just Bury the Son-of-a-Gun"

When Roy Rogers' horse died, he had Trigger stuffed and mounted and placed in a museum. Subsequently, when Gene Autry's horse, Champion, died, Gene said to his wife, Jackie, "I want to do what Roy did. I want to have Champion stuffed and mounted." And she said, "It cost him $50,000 to do that." I don't know what the exact figure was. Autry said, "It did? Well, just bury the son-of-a-gun."